ROBOTS

**Tamara Hartson
& Super Explorers**

What is a Robot?

A **robot** is any kind of machine that has sensors, receives instructions from a person, makes a decision and carries out those instructions. Even a printer is a type of **robot**!

Robots come in many shapes and sizes. Some even have faces, arms and legs and look a lot like people. But most robots do not look like people at all!

Robots can only do what we program them to do. Some robots play soccer. Other robots conduct scientific experiments in space!

Parts of a Robot

Robots have sensors that can help them "see," "hear" and "feel." This robot has cameras for its "eyes."

ASIMO

HONDA

Robots need to be able to do things. They have "hands" or "arms" or some other way to handle objects.

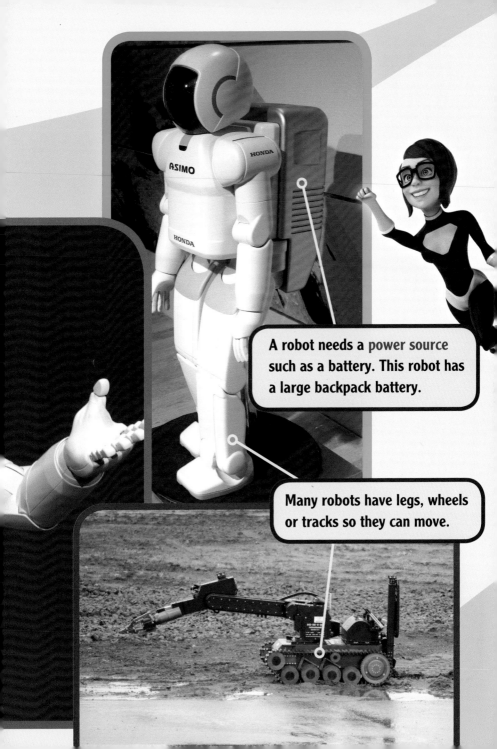

A robot needs a power source such as a battery. This robot has a large backpack battery.

Many robots have legs, wheels or tracks so they can move.

Actuators

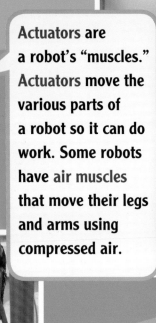

Actuators are a robot's "muscles." Actuators move the various parts of a robot so it can do work. Some robots have air muscles that move their legs and arms using compressed air.

This is a robot named Baxter. It can be trained to perform jobs. If you move its arms to do a task, it will learn the movement and repeat the task by itself.

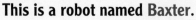

Most robots have electric motors that turn gears to move their arms or working parts.

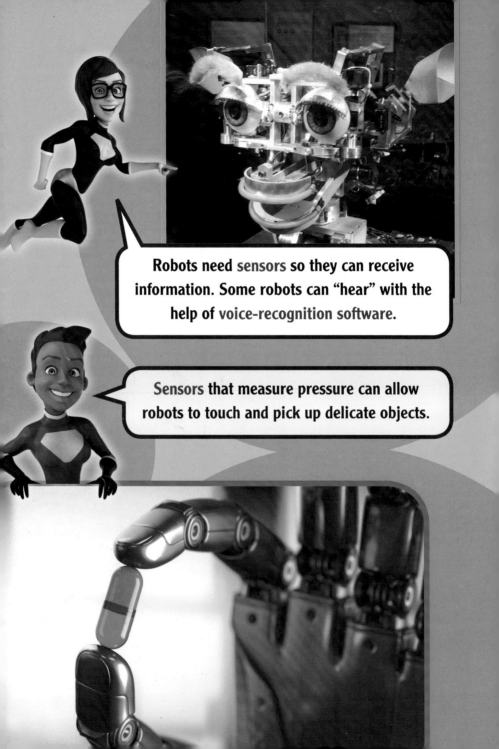

Robots need sensors so they can receive information. Some robots can "hear" with the help of voice-recognition software.

Sensors that measure pressure can allow robots to touch and pick up delicate objects.

Sensors

Some robots use cameras that measure light to help the robot "see." They can detect movement and some can recognize human faces.

Manipulation

Robots are built to be able to do work. Some robots have hands, but unlike human hands, robot hands are not very good at grabbing and moving things. Most robots have other manipulators such as claws, drills, or suction cups.

Robotic hands have been built to help people who have lost their hands or arms in accidents.

Suction cups work well for jobs such as lifting boxes. Many suctions cups together can lift heavy objects.

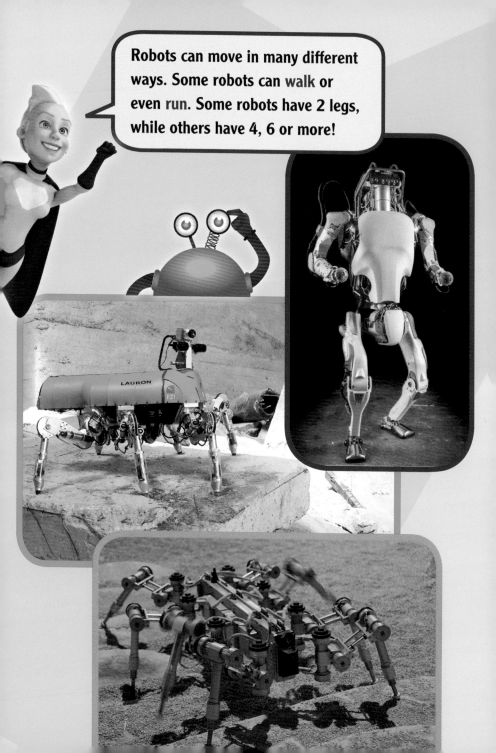

Robots can move in many different ways. Some robots can walk or even run. Some robots have 2 legs, while others have 4, 6 or more!

Locomotion

Some robots have wheels; some have fins. Some can fly, while others float. Robots can move in any way we can imagine!

Science Fiction

Robots often appear in science fiction books and movies. The author Isaac Asimov wrote many stories about robots and even made up the word "robotics." Robots in science fiction often can do much more than robots in present-day real life.

Isaac Asimov

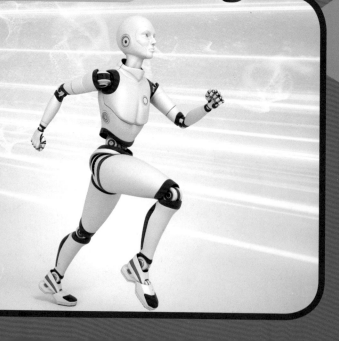

A robotic R2-D2 replica

A person in a replica C-3PO costume

Two of the most famous robots in science fiction are R2-D2 and C-3PO from the Star Wars movies. Both R2-D2 and C-3PO are actually actors in costumes; neither are real robots!

The First Robots

People have been inventing robots for a long time. More than 2000 years ago a Greek mathematician and inventor named Archytas created a steam-operated bird that he called The Pigeon. Because it flew by itself, this invention is said to be one of the first robots.

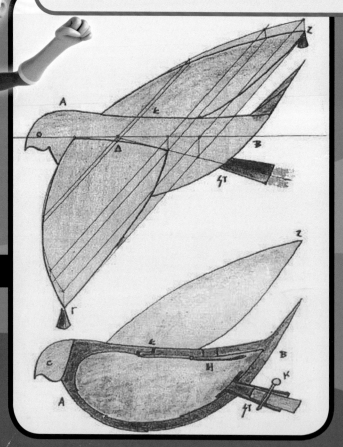

The Pigeon

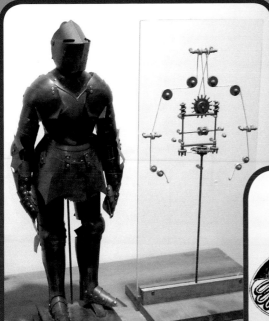

Leonardo's Robot

Mechanical Duck

George

More than 500 years ago Leonardo da Vinci invented a mechanical knight that could sit up and move its arms, head and jaw. Around 1930 William Richards made George, another metal robot. A more complex robot was the Mechanical Duck, invented by Jacques de Vaucanson in the 1700s. It could flap its wings, eat and even poop!

Al-Jazari's Automata

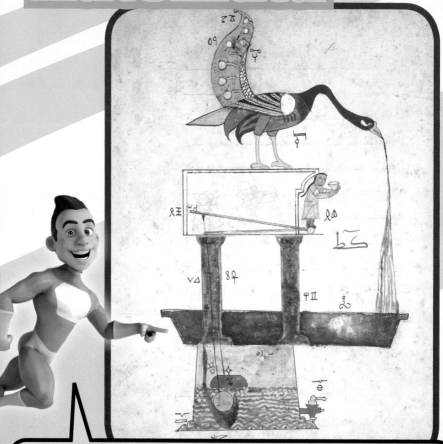

Al-Jazari was an inventor, mathematician and artist who lived more than 800 years ago. He created some of the world's first robots. He called them automata. There was no electricity at the time, so he used water to move many of his robots.

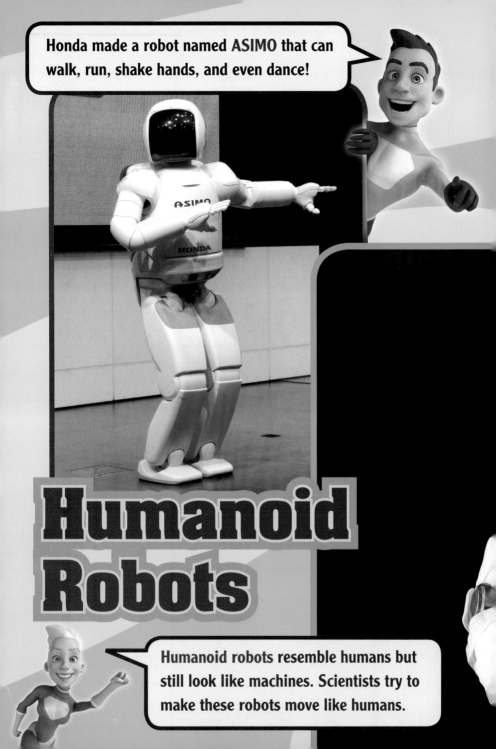

Honda made a robot named ASIMO that can walk, run, shake hands, and even dance!

Humanoid Robots

Humanoid robots resemble humans but still look like machines. Scientists try to make these robots move like humans.

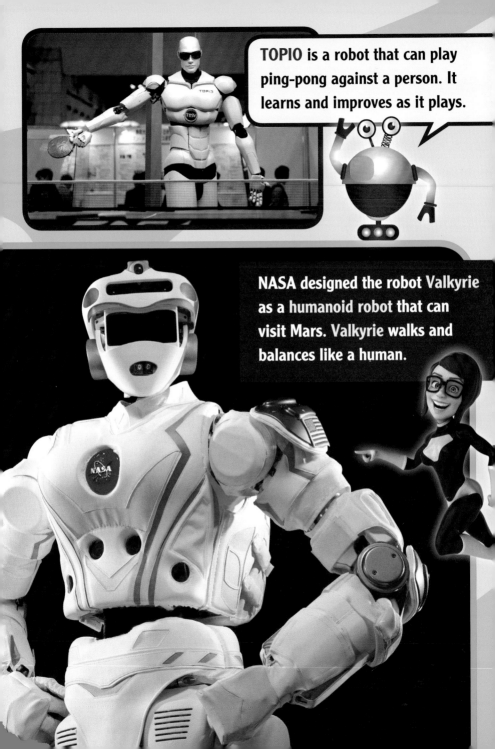

TOPIO is a robot that can play ping-pong against a person. It learns and improves as it plays.

NASA designed the robot Valkyrie as a humanoid robot that can visit Mars. Valkyrie walks and balances like a human.

Androids

Androids are humanoid robots that are made to look as much like humans as possible. Unlike other humanoid robots, androids do not yet walk or move well. When building an android scientists want to create human-like facial expressions, head movements and the ability to talk and respond to questions. The majority of androids are made in Japan, Korea and China.

Androids have motors and a power source that are outside their bodies and connected by hidden cables. **Androids** cannot move on their own.

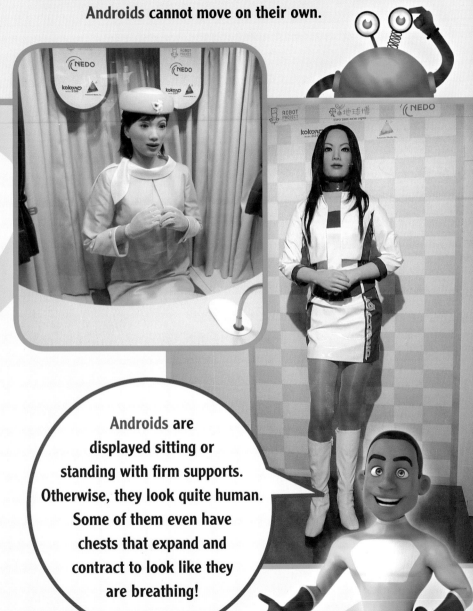

Androids are displayed sitting or standing with firm supports. Otherwise, they look quite human. Some of them even have chests that expand and contract to look like they are breathing!

Industrial Robots

Industrial robots are machines that can be programmed to do certain tasks. Although they don't look like robots, they are! Many industrial robots are mechanical arms that work on assembly lines.

What is a robot's favourite type of music?

Heavy metal.

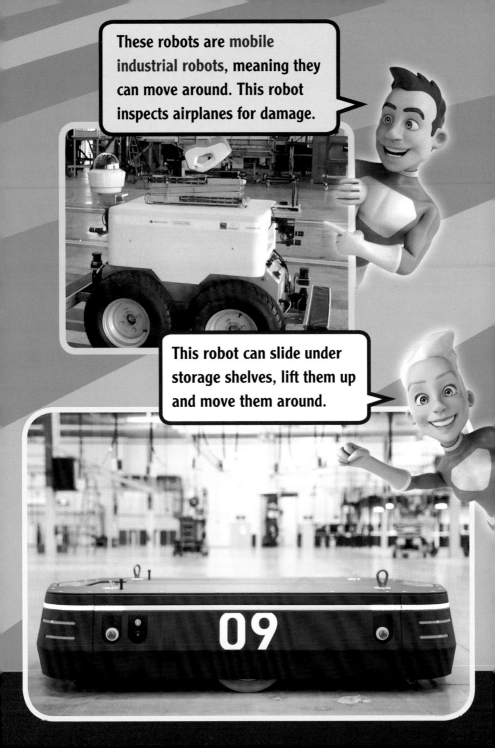

Nanorobots

Nanorobotics is the science of creating very tiny microscopic robots. Nanorobots or nanites are only in the early stages of development. The first working nanorobot is a microscopic sensor that can count molecules.

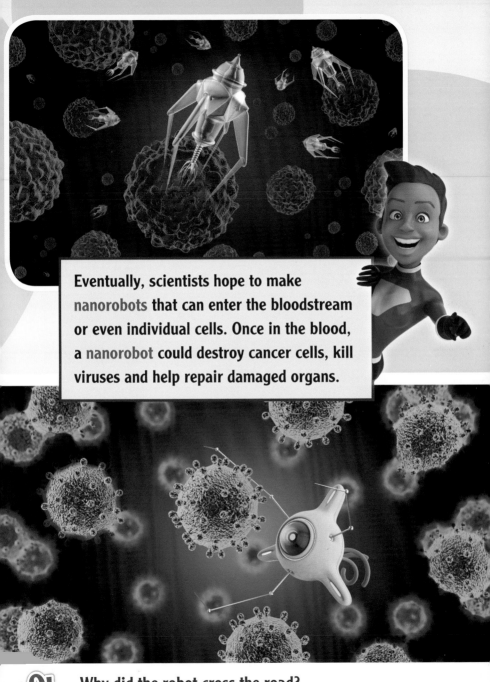

Eventually, scientists hope to make nanorobots that can enter the bloodstream or even individual cells. Once in the blood, a nanorobot could destroy cancer cells, kill viruses and help repair damaged organs.

Why did the robot cross the road?

It was programmed by the chicken.

Robots in Space

Every probe and vehicle sent into space is a kind of robot.
Rovers are vehicles that have been sent to the moon and Mars.
NASA has a new **rover** called **ATHLETE**. It has 6 legs and will be
used on the moon to carry heavy objects such as machinery and
research pods. It is still being tested in deserts on Earth.

The two **Voyager** space probes were launched in 1977 and have now left the outer Solar System. They continue to send data about interstellar space.

Voyager I

The probe **Huygens** landed on Saturn's moon **Titan** and sent images of the surface.

Huygens

Huygens photo of Titan's surface

NASA has even created **humanoid robotic astronauts** that could be sent to Mars before humans make the trip.

Educational Robots

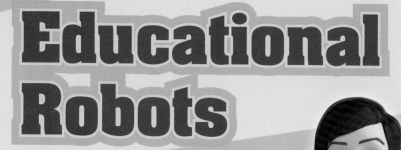

Robots can be used in classrooms to help teach mathematics, physics, programming, and electronics. Students that are really good at building and programming robots can enter robot competitions.

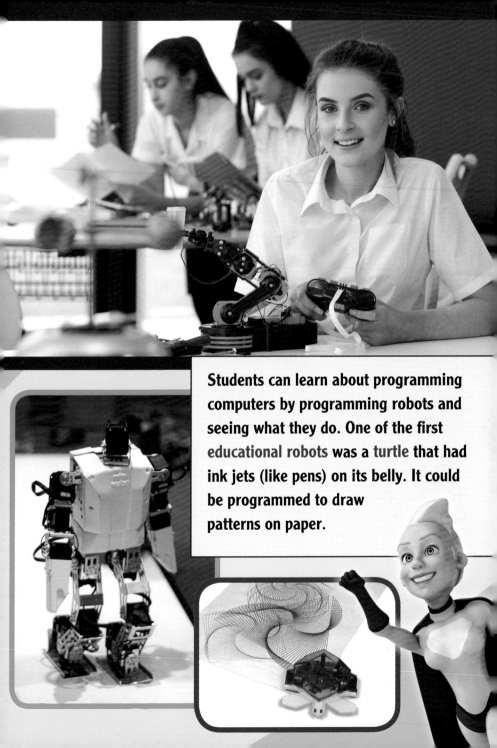

Students can learn about programming computers by programming robots and seeing what they do. One of the first educational robots was a turtle that had ink jets (like pens) on its belly. It could be programmed to draw patterns on paper.

Military robots can be simple vehicles that carry cameras into dangerous areas or unmanned drones that help with research, delivery or combat.

Military
Robots

These 2 robots were designed to carry supplies for soldiers.
They can move quickly up hills and over rough ground.
Both of these robots are powered by gasoline engines.

Bomb Detection

Both the military and police use bomb detection robots. These robots can inspect suspicious packages and bombs without putting any people in danger.

This robot is called Dragon Runner. It has cameras to send live video to military specialists who can use the robot to disarm a bomb.

Flying Robots

Flying robots are called drones or UAVs, which stands for Unmanned Aerial Vehicle. Drones can be used for surveillance, delivering packages or doing research or photography.

A robot walks into a coffee shop, orders a drink, and lays down some cash. The server says, "Hey, we don't serve robots." The robot says, "Oh, but someday you will."

LOL

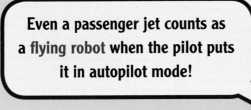

Even a passenger jet counts as a flying robot when the pilot puts it in autopilot mode!

Although drones were first developed for the military, regular people can now own small drones like this one. These drones far outnumber the drones used by the military.

Underwater Robots

Special robots designed to handle water and pressure are called underwater robots. These robots can go deep underwater to repair oil and gas equipment, do scientific research or collect samples.

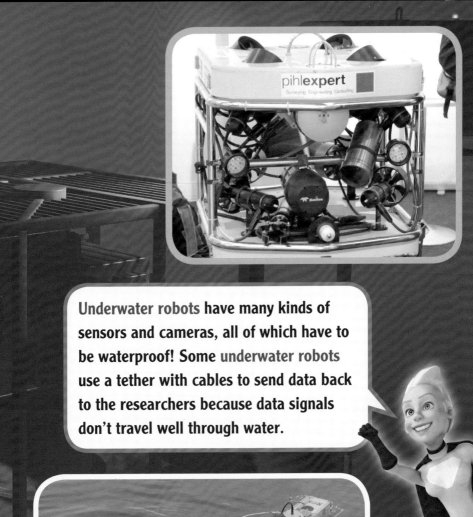

Underwater robots have many kinds of sensors and cameras, all of which have to be waterproof! Some underwater robots use a tether with cables to send data back to the researchers because data signals don't travel well through water.

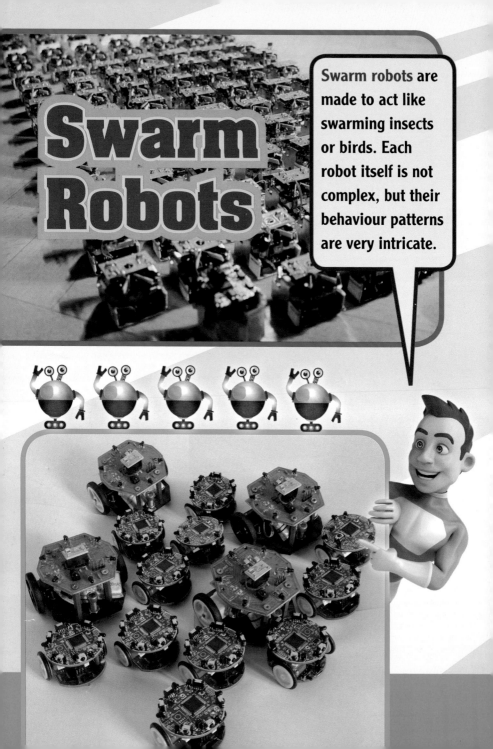

Swarm Robots

Swarm robots are made to act like swarming insects or birds. Each robot itself is not complex, but their behaviour patterns are very intricate.

Creating and studying swarm robots helps us understand how individuals cooperate with others as well as how the swarm works as a whole. This gives us a better understanding of artificial swarm intelligence.

What did the man say to his dead robot?

Rust in peace.

Animal Robots

People who build robots often study animal movement so they can make animal robots, such as this robotic snake. Pleo, a robotic dinosaur, walks and moves its head and tail in the way we imagine a dinosaur would move.

Some **animal robots** are toys that respond to commands and learn. There's even a toy mouse for cats that gets itself out of corners and turns itself over if it lands on its back!

Security Robots

Security robots can monitor buildings and other property to prevent criminal activity.

Security robots have cameras to record activity. Some are able to speak basic sentences such as, "Stop! You are being recorded!"

This security robot is part of a police force in Russia. It has 5 cameras to record crimes on city streets.

Medical Robots

One of the most important medical robots is the laparoscopic robot. The surgeon controls the robot and watches the surgery on a magnified screen instead of using the laparoscopic tools directly. Surgeries done with robotic systems are faster with less tissue damage and faster healing times.

This seal is a **therapy robot**. It moves, responds to being petted and can learn names. It can relieve depression for many patients in hospitals.

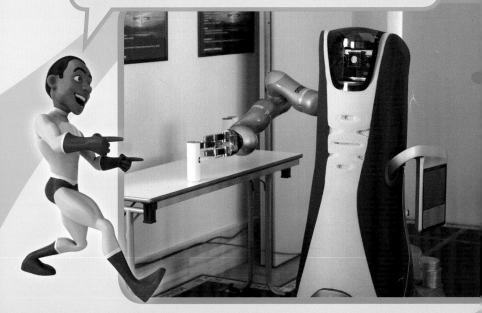

The **CareBot** can help patients in hospitals or in their own homes. It can carry things, serve drinks and food and alert a doctor in case of an emergency.

Scientific Robots

Some robots are built to gather scientific data, especially in high risk areas. This is Dante, a robot that can enter volcanic craters to take samples and measurements.

NASA builds many robots to do research on the moon or other planets. This is K10, a rover that may go to the moon.

NASA also built SnoMote, a small snowmobile robot that can explore Earth's polar ice caps.

Agricultural robots help with planting, harvesting and food storage. The robot above moves plants in a greenhouse. The robot in the photo below plants seedlings.

Agricultural Robots

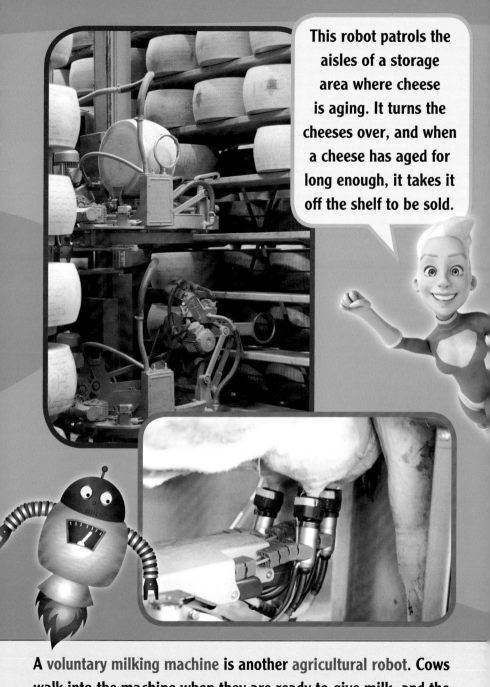

This robot patrols the aisles of a storage area where cheese is aging. It turns the cheeses over, and when a cheese has aged for long enough, it takes it off the shelf to be sold.

A voluntary milking machine is another agricultural robot. Cows walk into the machine when they are ready to give milk, and the robotic machine hooks itself up and begins milking the cow.

Household Robots

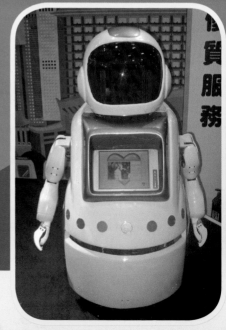

One of the first and most useful household robots is the robotic vacuum. It cleans the floors and learns the floorplan of your house. Some housekeeping robots such as the one on the right have a vacuum built into the base.

Like the robotic vacuum, pool robots are able to learn the shape of the pool to clean the entire bottom without any help.

A lawn mower robot is a quiet and efficient robot that can mow your lawn on a set schedule, even at night! Some are even solar powered.

Modular Robots

Modular robots are small robots that combine together to make a larger robot. These individual robots can recombine in different shapes depending on what the robot needs to do.

This modular robot can change shape to have many arms like an octopus, two legs like a person or no arms or legs at all like a snake!

Modular robots usually have several points of attachment so they can hook up to each other in various ways. These are some of the most adaptable of all robots.

Autonomous Things

Autonomous things refers to machines and robots that are able to work or move without direction from humans. These robots have excellent learning abilities or artificial intelligence (AI).

Why was the robot angry?
Because someone kept pushing his buttons.

This drone is self-navigating. It delivers food to a man living in the mountains of eastern Portugal.

Self-driving cars and self-navigating drones are two kinds of autonomous things. Cars that drive themselves are much safer than cars driven by people. In the future, many researchers hope all cars will be autonomous.

Each year, many competitions are held where robots show off their skills. Ball games, obstacle courses and races are some of the ways in which robots compete.

Competitions

Robot soccer is a big attraction for engineers, students and researchers. Soccer-playing robots need to have good balance and the ability to learn and adapt to the game.

Nao robots, like this one, are excellent soccer players!

Robot Combat

Robot combat is meant to be educational and fun. Engineering and robotics students build robots with saws and hammers attached to them in order to destroy other robots in a competition. Robot combat helps researchers understand robot movement and stability.

Here are more robots specially design to combat one another.

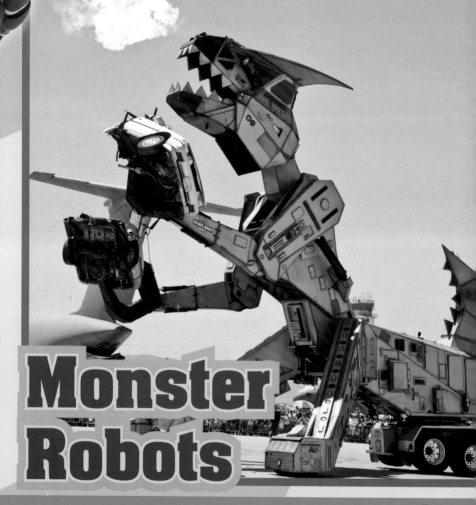

Robosaurus is one of the largest robots ever built. It breathes fire and can break cars in half! **Robosaurus** is controlled by a driver sitting in the head.

Monster Robots

What do you call a pirate robot?

Arrrrr2D2.

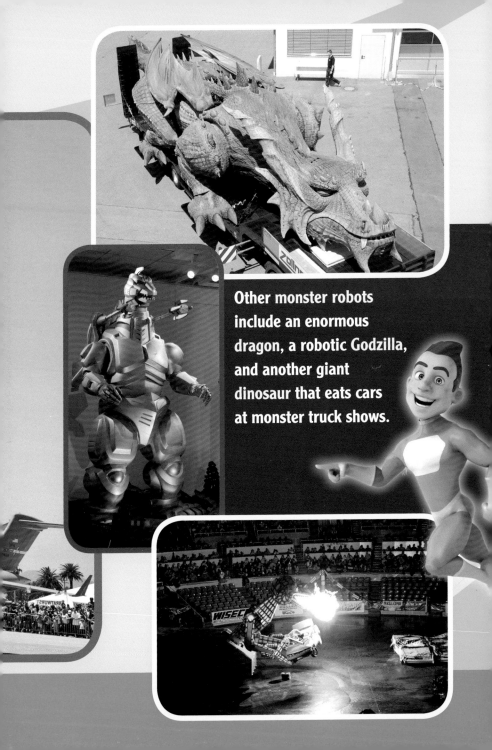

Other monster robots include an enormous dragon, a robotic Godzilla, and another giant dinosaur that eats cars at monster truck shows.

The Publisher: Mega Machines is an imprint of Blue Bike Books

Library and Archives Canada Cataloguing in Publication

Hartson, Tamara, 1974–, author
Robots / Tamara Hartson & Super Explorers

Issued in print and electronic formats.
ISBN 978-1-926700-83-0 (softcover)
ISBN 978-1-926700-84-7 (epub)

1. Robots—Juvenile literature. I. Super Explorers (Children's author), author II. Title.

| TJ211.2.H37 2017 | j629.8'92 | C2017-906437-1 |
| | | C2017-906438-X |

Frontcover: Robot engineer: Ociacia/Thinkstock.

Backcover: Thunder_Over_The_Empire_Airfest-Tech. Sgt. Joselito Aribuabo; robocup-Ralf Roletschek; Dante-CMU Field Robotics Center (FRC)/NASA.

Photo Credits: 3DetectionLabs 45b; Aaron Biggs 47a; Abteilung IDS 9b, 12b; agnormark/Thinkstock 37b; Alex Healing 61c; Anders Sandberg 6b; asuscreative 41b; AZAdam 9a; Bundesarchiv, Bild 102-13018/CC-BY-SA 3.0 17c; Cédric Bonhomme 43b; Charles Haynes 61a; Chesky_W/Thinkstock 10c; Chris6/Thinkstock 51b; ClaudioVentrella/Thinkstock 51a; coffeekai/Thinkstock 52a; curtoicurto/Thinkstock 53a; Daniel Schwen 63c; DARPA 33b; Dave Subelack 37a; David Buckley 6a; David Monniaux 29b; davincidig/Thinkstock 2–3; DGLimages/Thinkstock 31a; Dkroetsch 13e; Dr. Karl-Heinz Hochhaus 39a; Eduardofamendes 57; Eneas De Troya 59a; Farshadarvin 40b; Francesco Mondada and Michael Bonani 54; FRC/NASA 48a; Gadlopes 13b; Georgia Institute of Technology 49b; Gnsin 23b; Highwaystarz-Photography/Thinkstock 30; http://www.kansascity.com/news/business/technology/917xpi/picture62197987/ALTERNATES/FREE_640/atlas%20from%20boston%20dynamics 12a; Humanrobo 21a; Humanrobo 21a; Hunini 63b; ICAPlants 24; iLexx /Thinkstock 14b; Intel Free Press 44c; Jared C. Benedict 8a; Jdietsch 44a; Jennifer 23a; Jes80 60; Jiuguang Wang 13c, 31b, 41a, 47b; ktsimage/Thinkstock 8b, 26; kynny/Thinkstock 7a; Les Chatfield 61b; LSDSL 5a; Luc Jaulin 13d; M P Hennessey 25b; Marco Verch 15a; Markyim 55c; MattiPaavola 45a; Max Braun 22; Mhrobots 50a; Momotarou2012 20a; monstArrr_/Thinkstock 10a; NASA 20–21, 28a, 28b, 29a, 29c, 29d; NASA/JPL-Caltech 48b; Nimur 46; pablo_rodriguez1/Thinkstock 50b; Pedro ximenez 63a; PhonlamaiPhoto/Thinkstock 10b; pixone/Thinkstock 38–39; porpeller/Thinkstock 53b; Ralf Roletschek 59b; Richard Greenhill and Hugo Elias 11a; Rico Shen 52b; Robocluster 55a; Sergey Kornienko 40a; Stanislas Larnier 25a; Star Wars/flickr 15b; Steve Dock/MOD 34–35; Steve Jurvetson 7b, 42a, 56; Stocktrek Images/Thinkstock 36; synaxonag 5b; Tamara Hartson 43a; Tech. Sgt. Joselito Aribuabo 62; Toyloverz 43c; Travis Isaacs 42b; twilightproductions/Thinkstock 44b; U.S. Air Force 32b; U.S. Navy 34b; Valiant Technology Ltd 31c; Vanillase 4; Volodymyr Horbovyy/Thinkstock 27b; wellphoto/Thinkstock 11b; wildpixel/Thinkstock 27a; Милан Јелисавчић 55b.

Superhero Illustrations: julos/Thinkstock.

Robot Illustrations: studiogstock/Thinkstock.

Produced with the assistance of the Government of Alberta, Alberta Media Fund.

Alberta
Government

We acknowledge the financial support of the Government of Canada.
Nous reconnaissons l'appui financier du gouvernement du Canada.

Funded by the Government of Canada
Financé par le gouvernement du Canada

Canadä

PC: 38